Kiddy inks
writing & illustrating programme

lizzie reaches the rainbow

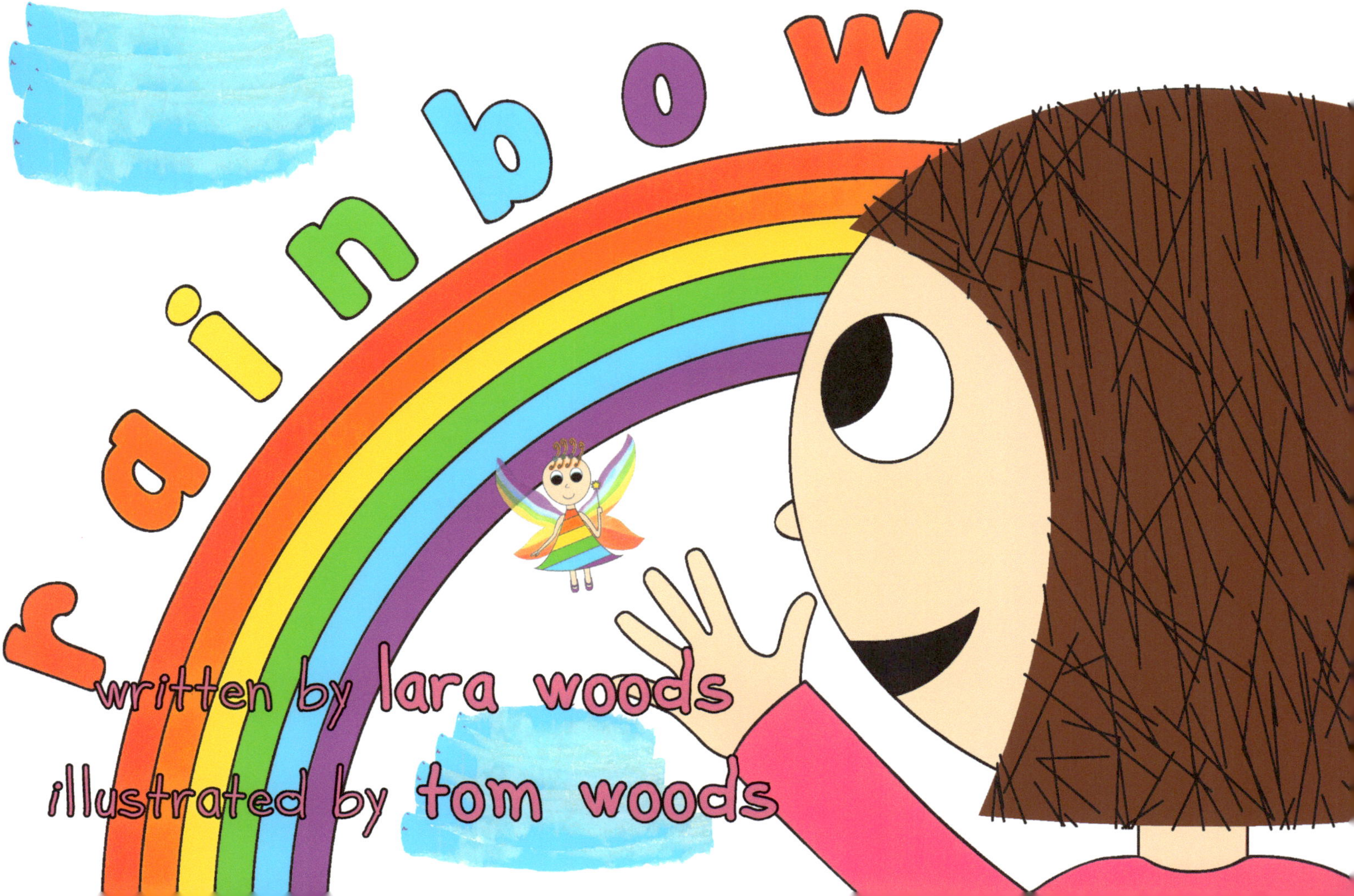

written by lara woods
illustrated by tom woods

Stop it! Just stop it! Lizzie thought.

She listened to arguing and crying coming from downstairs while her parents had another fight. They fought almost every day.

Lizzie's mum would cry. Lizzie's dad would shout. Lizzie would hide in her room, while her cat **Ginger** snuggled and purred in her arms.

Today, Lizzie wished she could escape. She pulled open the **lacy curtains** and peeked outside. It had just stopped raining and a hazy **rainbow** stretched wide across the sky. 'How peaceful it would be at that **rainbow**,' Lizzie thought.

Later that night, when she was tucked in her bed and all the fighting had stopped, Lizzie looked through her window again. She wished on the twinkly stars that she could visit the rainbow one day.

Lizzie fell asleep with a smile, imagining herself in a magical rainbow world with glitter-bright colours, where she would always be happy.

Bright and early the next morning, Lizzie heard a **tap, tap, tap** on her window.
She rubbed her eyes and looked outside. A person as tiny as a toothpick, with transparent, silky wings and a wispy **rainbow**-coloured dress, was holding a shimmering wand.

A fairy!

Lizzie opened her window and the fairy flew straight into her bedroom and fluttered around, looking at Lizzie with **sparkling blue eyes**.

The fairy had a cheeky smile on her tiny face. 'First fairy you've seen, hey?' she said.

Lizzie nodded, with her mouth wide open.

'My name's Imogen,' the fairy said. 'I heard your wish. It's my job to answer to all rainbow wishes, you see.'

With that, Imogen waved her wand at Lizzie. Before Lizzie could blink, she was flying **higher** and **higher**!

'Well, what do you think about that?' Imogen looked pleased with herself.

'I'm flying! I'm flying!' Lizzie laughed.

'You sure are,' Imogen laughed back. 'Come on, we have a **rainbow** to explore!'

Imogen and Lizzie flew out the window and up, up, up into the sky. Together, they flew towards the magical rainbow.

'Here we are,' Imogen said.
Lizzie couldn't see Imogen anywhere. Where was she?
Everything was red!
Finally, Lizzie spotted Imogen flitting around the red haze.
'Lizzie, what are some of your favourite red things?' Imogen asked.
'Ooh, I love **red apples** and **red roses**,' Lizzie said. In a flash, sparkly *images* of *juicy* apples and lovely roses danced all around the red sea. It was breathtaking.
'Lizzie,' Imogen said softly, 'red *is* for **Resilience**. Whenever you need resilience, just remember this moment.'
'I will,' said Lizzie.

Imogen buzzed around Lizzie's head. 'Follow me!' she called.

This time they flew into a bright orange world.

'Wow!' Lizzie marvelled.

'Which orange things do you love?' Imogen asked.

'Delicious **orange juice** and **Ginger, my cat**, of course,' Lizzie said, smiling at the thought of her snuggly cat.

'Great! Orange is for **Optimism.** When you need to be optimistic, just remember this magical moment.' Lizzie nodded.

Next they flew through yellow, where Imogen shouted, 'This is my favourite colour!' and Lizzie thought of her favourite things which were **sunny daffodils** and **mushy bananas**.

Lizzie promised to remember Imogen's words: 'Yellow is for **Yourself**. Always believe in yourself, Lizzie.'

And on *it* went, as they flew through green ...
"**Slimy frogs** and **tall trees**!" exclaimed Lizzie.

"**Generosity**!" cheered Imogen.

And blue ... where Lizzie's favourite blue things – **small, round blueberries** and her **fluffy toy, Boo Bear** – danced in the blue haze, and Imogen taught her about **Bravery.**

And last of all, they flew through a spectacular sea of purple, Lizzie's favourite colour in the whole world. **Sweet-smelling lavender** and **crisp grapes** floated around her, as Imogen told her to remember the word **Peace**.

All too soon, the rainbow began to fade.

'Time to go, Lizzie,' Imogen said.

They flew through blue skies and gentle winds all the way back to Lizzie's open bedroom window.

'That was UNBELIEVABLE!' Lizzie beamed.
Imogen smiled. 'Lizzie, everything *is* believable *if* you believe *it* enough,' she said. 'You wanted peace that the rainbow would bring. You believed *in* me and your wish, and *it* came true. Anything you believe *is* possible. So from now on, any time you need to find that peace, just remember our special moments *in* the rainbow . Close your eyes and believe *it* all over again. You won't even need me.'

'But I will need you.' Lizzie's bottom lip trembled.
Imogen fluttered closer to Lizzie and landed on her hands.

'Instead of Imogen, you will have your very own **Imagination** to take you to the rainbow, and once you pass through every colour and remember all your favourite things and all the special things that you already are, that peace will come back to you every time. I promise!'

'I believe your promise,' Lizzie said.

'Take care Lizzie, and don't forget, you can always reach the rainbow.'

Imogen fairy-kissed Lizzie's forehead and flew out the window into night sky.

And the next time Lizzie felt like she needed to escape to the rainbow for some peace, that's exactly what she did!

Our annual KiddyInks programme aims to nurture young writing and illustrating talent, and offers Australian primary school children in Years 3-6 the opportunity to create a picture book.
We aim to roll this programme out annually to selected schools.

If you would like further information about our KiddyInks programme or if you are interested in becoming a sponsor you can
email: publisher@serenitypress.org
www.serenitypress.org

Meet our 2016 KiddyInks author and illlustrator

Lara Woods is thirteen-years-old and the biggest bookworm around! Lara grew up on fairy stories, wizard stories and all kinds of magical books. Lara loves dancing and she especially loves her role as an assistant dance teacher to little ones. She plays piano and guitar, she sings in the school choir, she dreams of becoming a world famous actress one day and whenever she has a spare minute, she can be found writing fan-fiction of her favourite novels or cuddling up with her cat, Meggy.

Tom Woods is sixteen-years-old and the equal biggest bookworm around! Tom has been drawing since he could hold a crayon and he loves to draw anything from new Mario game characters to his dream cars. Tom loves Aussie Rules Football almost as much as he loves art and has been playing footy for the same team since he was seven-years-old. Tom dreams of being a designer for Pixar or Lego or Ferrari or all three! In his spare time you'll find Tom on his skateboard with his dog, Hercules, running behind him or down at the beach where he comes up with his ideas of what to draw next.

Dedication

For Mum and Dad who gave me my wings and for Mrs Knox and Miss K who taught me how to fly - Lara.

To Mum and Dad who showed me that art was as important as maths and to Mr Garrity who inspires creativity in me every day - Tom

Serenity Press
Waikiki, WA 6169

First published by Serenity Press (Serenity Kids) in 2016
www.serenitypress.org

Copyright Lara Woods 2016

All rights reserved. No part of this publication may be reproduced, stored in a retrieval system, or transmitted in any form or by any mean, electronic, mechanical, photocopying, recording or otherwise, without the prior written permission of the publisher.

National Library of Australia
Cataloguing in-Publication entry

Woods, Lara, Lara Woods
Lizzie Reaches the Rainbow

ISBN 978-0-9953976-0-6 (sc)
978-0-9953976-1-3 (eBook)
978-0-9953976-2-0 (hc)

1. Family- parents– Juvenile fiction. 2. Fairytale and folklore– Juvenile fiction.
3 Action and adventure survival stories– Juvenile fiction.

Cover and illustrations by Tom Woods
Printed and bound by Lightning Source Ltd

www.ingramcontent.com/pod-product-compliance
Lightning Source LLC
Chambersburg PA
CBHW041125300426
44113CB00002B/60